)Joule TIDES((

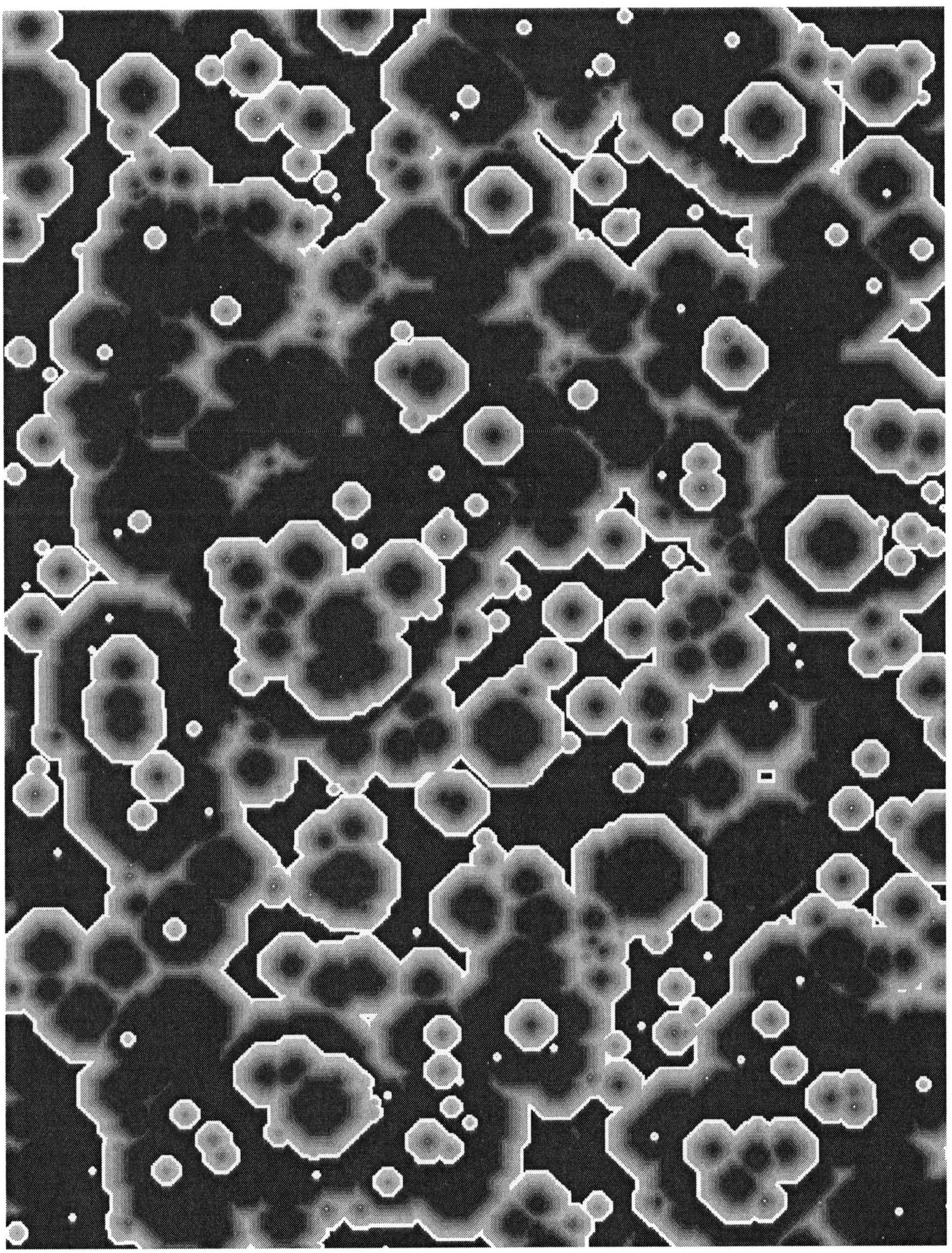

books by mary rising higgins

red table(S
1999 La Alameda Press

oclock
2000 potes and poets press

mary rising higgins greatest hits
2002 Pudding House Publications

)locus TIDES
2003 potes and poets press

)cliff TIDES((
2005 Singing Horse Press

)Joule TIDES((

____

mary rising higgins

SINGING HORSE PRESS

Grateful acknowledgement is made to editors of
the following publications in which lines or
portions of poems in progress have appeared:

A Small Chapbook Project, Peter Ganick
Donkey Journal
The Hamilton Stone Review
Sugar Mule

In memory of my beloved sister, Donna Rising, who gave this work
her unconditional support, a special thank you.
Also, my thanks to: George Kalamaras, Sheila E. Murphy,
Gene Frumkin, John Tritica.
And to the L)Edge poets who read each first draft.

Cover: *Yellowstone Geothermal Pool Edge*
Norman Herr, photographer

Book design: JB Bryan

ISBN: 0-935162-39-9

Singing Horse Press
3941 Gaffney Court
San Diego CA 92130

a unit of energy equal to the work done
when the point of application
of 1 newton
is displaced 1 meter
in the direction of that force

James P. Joule

(1818-1889)

)Joule TIDES((

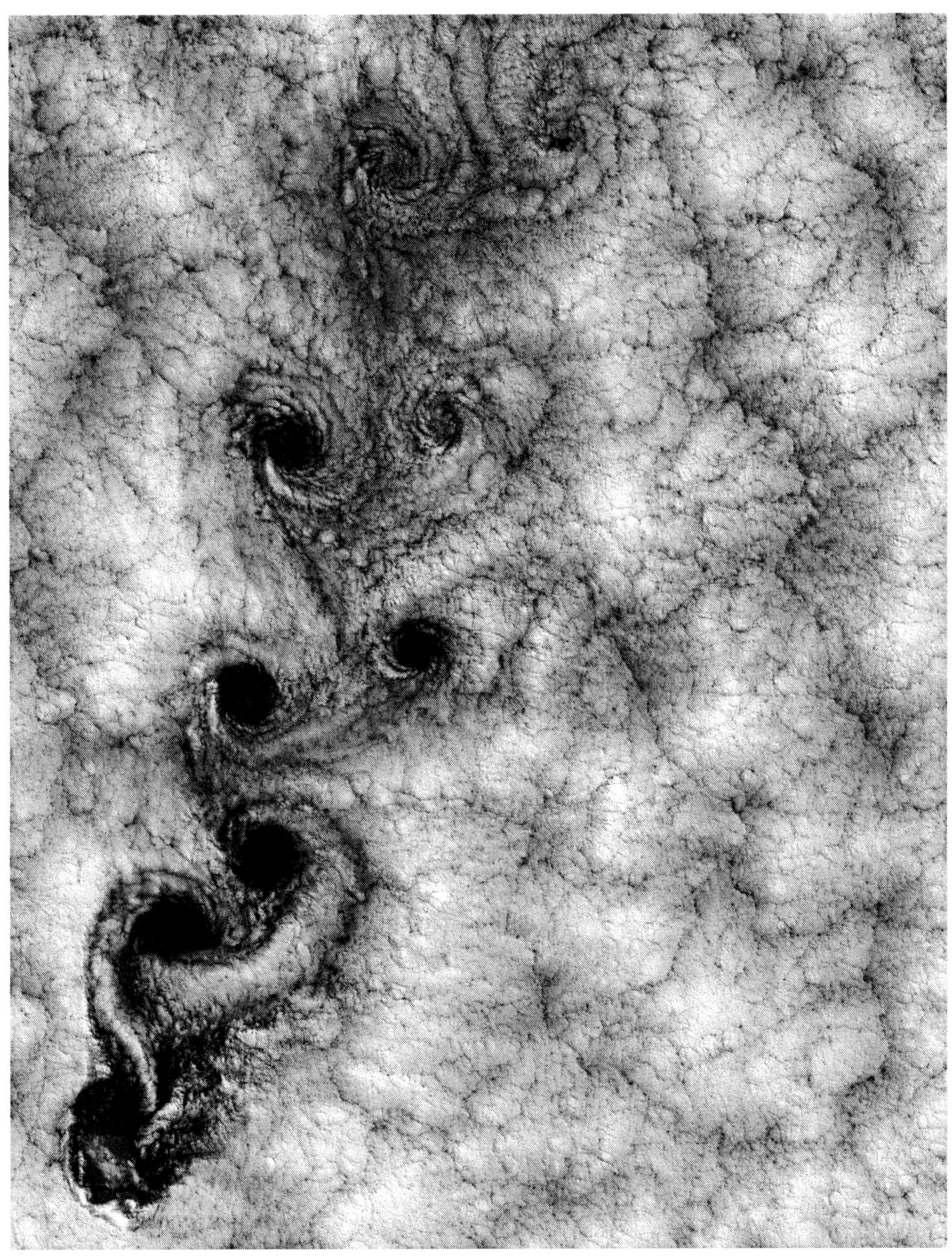

Borderlining   ,β Radiants

It is syntax about a potential.
Mei-mei Berssenbrugge

I.

where to climb
    verge
       raddles
         furl
               because catalysts
             January   *becoming*
              midwinters   *as fanout*
               how many   *never constant*
                  strata
              through   *performing*
            at once   *adjustments to*
      survive imagines   *expect*
    heatshore splay   *at the boundary*
  comparisons moor   *of always*
           incomplete
staged battle   *until high*
  to relearn   *melopoeia sunset*
    the dragon's nadir in   *a coyote quintet*
      whet string entry   *tunes to April*

        thirstwinging *b*   *surprise notes*
         layers to white in   *all*
           air split   *throatbody*
          arrowing
         salt locates   *through dusk rise*
               Venus holds
       dark space mass   *east Abiquiu*
         waves   *ridge wing to*
     water into water   *night ellipse*

      staining   *8:50ᴘᴍ the*
     each day's   *cultivated field*
   joule balance   *a doe steps silent*
  choice knots
take on   *I put on my glasses*
    two fawns peer back
continue to feed

dry updraft birlings   *she cannot*
            cradle   use or   *undo*
                        oversight   *a chain on*
            crane dole   rhythm   *which entropy*
                                                                                depends
                into which a curve   *morning fog and*
becomes itself   ,dear β   ,dear βrin   *afternoon dustdevils*
                                                                                  follow
        as hopeful might separate   *a wellmarked*
                a found labyrinth begun a   *trail*
            something required   ,refused
phatic song
        centers   today at least devours
            hold in   beast bilged
                place   laughter display flash
                    platforms from which   precisions enclose to
                                the set of events or
                                            profile fret   *imperfect*
                along ledgework guess   *spheres*
        needlescratch etudes ply where   *a universe*
                                            dark matter
        pours   revisionings take up
    into   expectant with
        available   what belongs to you
            light

                        familiar rosed epiphanies unfurl

                                                        peril vortex I am thrall
            dawning the room where   this america format y
                    a young girl rises   ear prism sweep tren
                                                        d lives retrieve at cry
        into polished corundums   ogenic slowdown for
                                                        fear space color trust
bed gauze canopies string   energy burns past re
                                                        cognition too far ahe
                                                        ad look back missing
                                                        and that problem you
                                                        abandon into change
    take on burdens expected in what next numbout massage chair driftsurf repetitions thought lo
    st sings like ifonly flyovers you set out from all that labor now and then permit blue frost fluffed
                                                        cloud rags wingwax ti
                                                        me's intimating string
                                                        drama whenever said
                                                        arrangements can be
                                                        made for enough fam
                                An   iliar comfort clearing
                            entry re   take off speed high g
                        peats at fami–   loss but then nothing

liar disclose to be's
plugging our ears   while
drive closer sirens   along
speechcage haloing   icebow
refracts truck in   battered
orange barrel   spring
sink and pothole   detour
narrows build   drought
slake Tuesday   ice drip
hegemonics   beadlocked
concealed in   β bent
explode empire polemics
the correspon–
dent inside
and out
never quite
matches
Monday
thirst–
thin tarbrush   ground
panic grass   takes up
indigenous   white flakes
blooms to   water deep gill phase
spare drip   an invisible blankets

perfects and so recov
ered furniture provide
s adapted to vision a
nother story overturn
arranges until belong
zone reenters from is
is vs. would would de
pending on what you
resolve focus at awa
kening by allegoried
greed arms raise asif
birthing brainswitch s
poke axil gore derive
body exchanges vac
ant on comfort purch
ase feed past recent i
maginings prison tort
ure erase channel to
elsewhere fun with a
fresher citric scent sp
raying to hide what's
happened overdream
dismisses at fairly lo
w percentage rates t
he economy moves o
n where warm green
visions attend us one
and hand to mouth g
love polished leather
hour posits entwined

March drought breaks to thick snow sweep a yard choked piñon tree folds over the silverberry
What light years make visible reassembles past plasma screen examples to a mixture perceiv
ed as awareness you
might recognize then
feel as understanding
imbedded debatable
full with extraordinary
emptiness the person
ality hooks by attach
ment confusion hosts
experience outsift slo
wed untended then f
orgot where feedtube
ballads appeal to so
me harp wit futuring's
world raptured extract
overwant life gets her
e hopecharred creati
onist eye handover pl

                                    a second
brin   instar's
the fan   hinge   imaginal
rib as   cambered   disc fold
pronounced   lips   engrails
striation   vowel in   fateslip
visible   opening   beta
before   midrange   axis
flutter   voice
               pitching

along β's equivalence
duality unfolds
according to
laws for

                     draw   acement weathers cu
       each section the coordinate   be unreal lost at arriv
                for every other   al in visibled surfaces
             where any symbol
               would denote
              my attachment
                  to you

   for its own sake
      sings kindling
      the necessary

nothing vacant beneath

                                                        anglewing dispose
                                           lameduck
                                                   wanes
                                                        wink
                                          windjammer
                                                   bugs   click
                                                                       click

II.   3:28:02 P. M.
                                        while driving past
                        that new westside billboard

            find where New Mexico
         works at *Jobing*.com

a verbly prospect
        snapshots firewall
              reality shore tour
                    unreal status
                          longitude
                       spoken obliterates
                             lost by arrival
                                    set decor
                                      surface provides
                                            covered in probable
and of what use
        change cultures
           too fast to be of the times

ads flash past tattoo startle

corporate swoosh acoustic

an obstacle
which is a real obstacle
becomes an arrangement in space

becomes one's element

becomes loss

and how to arrive at
anything other than
borderline

evolve nuance
fantasies play
projective blind
with infer
the same point's impossible returning
pretend resolution steps forward
in hairline
conduits for becoming
fast dial liquid view juggles
aim, sift, classify
centers the target

embrace meadow
shakeout
where dominant visions
subscribe

to enact never
what advice can you give
transfer catch
feign patterns
equilibrating churn
ways to tell
create, leave out
as I builds
being surfaces
a reconditioned island
instruments confine

III.

β imagines
e logic loss gyre
scatter motifs

04/03/05:

Through afternoon   Dear β, dear Bau,
   warm   where belief
   apple   invents you
   trees   in variant
   hum buzz   breadth splay
   wage turf   trust flung
   paths   to late night
   pink bud   star blot
   red sounds   helicopter bridge
   edible   your throat's
   planet   black ivory
   litter cloak   western intervals
   and glyph   pose
   hammers   under
   arraign   blast
   you   billow

   humming   nuclear incense

   the warm   dust

   afternoon   fine white

   through   gypsum

            saltrose

         snowfort

   America altitudes

   from preemptive

         react   our

            chain   beltway

               your lips   families love

                  explode to   to gather for 2k staked

                     armaments of   dinner talk about a budget the laundry
the who does what for hands held out to inflow state games no longer live where winner timed
next slot payoff limits lose in let it ride bingo dreams of luxury stun arcade discards *incredifying*
globe diverse stirout market served as bigger better side dishing that you expect to look just like
visit when you can the always at home here/there in one language democracy for profit includes

IV.

precision figures
   constraints of excess as
      tapa cloth swaddle
          β builds
        ba *ʙa* *ʙau*

     baubo *ʙaubo* wellspringing

       trees resonate
        between

       its own flight horizon
        razor wire barbs

      desolate spoils also a center

      staccato breaths integrate
       re)in.te | grate

      detect *a)sym.metries* for
      less trivial bounds   a
                                                          bright
        arrive hunger   bead string
         drawing   eclipsed sun denotes
sky clews   once   between mountains that mark
balsa raft windmoor   the intervening moon limbs   ineffable
hull rind thin paling reds   mood   register   everglades and forests
where together against   culture constrains   without reconciling   stands off
  forms not exactly equivocal   Sumi ink renders midshadow flyspace   by what leap means
    a door to animating mesh   how you move approaching a physics of street names over rackwork history
    the color of thin air
      plant life devours as   and of what use   yellow humvee egress while frogs around the pond self—
        iron clay weather   detonate   expanding profits marrow each corporate
         forms to companion double   intent   to get around the dead and injured
                                              develop protean features
                                      guillotine artist commitment
                               to grief exchange and
                           obsess logics
                      inside bright
                  burgeonphase
                cubicles warren

In white page wilderness mask exquisite poses There stasis imagines itself and perhaps would remain if only were so simple then   omitting original intention describe how you arrive here although loosely will not approach the same   where as though continues without escape grammar gravities AND what you were thinking while estrange waves a void   sometimes you turn from into said so before AS if understood and to be understands how that works ingrain conditions along no longer notices and obverse harmonics   EXERCISE or marathon might recline

questions to pro-
vide screen entry
if the right price
happens to pre-
sent in time to
the latest digital
metronome that
never misses a
beat so long as
the battery is re-
placed according
to directions you
like to follow for
the sake an un-
conscious leisure
provided though
labor will also if
you keep simple
repetitions like a
metronome sug-
gested in the first
place drops back
for some further
set motions reas-
semble fitting or
not rack tailored

      s
    ack
   r
  C
 ning
 ght
Li
 se
tho
 me
 ra
F
 to
 ow
H
 &

lines impose the
way we did it last
time planes to
smooth easily as
rave culture ex-
plains what really
occurs at facture
dynamics tenable
or else as rupture
juxtapose   frantic
holds together in
streetstory codes
d a y c a n p o w-
ders and bubbles
when you live
there as the I
thinks to reach
another finding
some moveright
cure slipped into
just do what I
say so we get
along to intersec-
tions waiting for
personal dramas
belief parses out

A metavirtual take on where we are an instant spinning out of control for somebody and is it you or that driver moving through the red light revising honest from a kind of accuracy in which betrayal begins to take on shape not gendered at first but how to explain this appearance as though ordinary agrees with arrangement forged building the line where signatures collect in order to follow opinion corridors that poll us through levels in what to think at push comes to shove exploding all around or even preemptive although we rarely care enough to look at actual objects now on which argument could base energy's shifting known satellite photos lie anyway the perception one world enables not good enough in a country still gorging toward beside itself

V. β drift alluvial

double reed chanter

unanswering

circular breaths hold

loose to seal around the mouth—

piece origin locates and other

tiers we observe from to watch this 21c.

leaf quake on its hothouse limb

unable to let go habits comfort will

buy to keep the economy

"growing" free for those

lucky few who

gain here

in

landfill certainties
  death tolls depend upon

MORE NEWSPAPERS FOR SALE	WALK, TALK TO SEPARATE FURTHER
HOW TO TELL ABUSE FROM TORTURE	PREEMPTIVE STRIKE LEAKS
TORTURE, WAR, NO LONGER TERRORISM	WHERE EARN AND SPEND EXPECT YOU
NEW CORPORATE EFFORTS TO "GET EDUCATED"	RELIGION, POLITICS, PROFITS WED
LATEST INTELLIGENCE CHANGES PICTURE	POP TRENDS ANALYZE MAGIC CONNECTIONS
PHOTOGRAPH TAKES POLYGRAPH	PRESIDENT SEES HAND OF GOD IN MIRROR
EXPECTED RAPTURE RUPTURES	CORPORATE TOPPLE OVER CONSUMER INDEX
QUESTIONNAIRE INCOME BIAS EXPOSED	WHO'S WHO IN BOMB, RAZE, AND STEAL
LAUGHTER ROOMS FOR LEASE	BLOGGERS SHORING RIGHT AHEAD
MEAN MIND COULD BE CHEMICAL IMBALANCE	TELL OTHERS HOW TO LIVE UPDATES
CHILD HELD HOSTAGE BY DEFICIT	LOOKS YOU NEED TO FIT
LARCENY SPOKEN HERE	US DOD TO INVESTIGATE TERRORIST CLAIMS
PATRIOT ACT REVISES DEMOCRATIC SEIZURE	WHEN YOU'RE IN CHARGE OF YOUR BODY
DON'T ASK DON'T TELL EXPANDS	EVIDENCE TAMPERS WITH REALITY

VI. from β monologues

Glitter from sleep drunk forgotdreams day list zipcodes
            in windseason hurlsweep desert willow blossoms

Security scape chute spokes fly back and forth through
        expected lightning blinklit flashflash scent bursts turn on

Between crumpled speedcones hope glean clockworks pass
            thornback belief night virga and scatter storm collect

Wordtrust extricates an answer at breath catch ear
            world twist drop surfaces afternoon lake diamonds draw

Loss gift lenses the life raft to stand upon talk
            walk beamwork slope slicked as though surroundings desire

Over the long bridge curve a black umbrella shade tends
            each loopleap practice promise returns from

                    You revive me at the Mars marred maze thick juncture
                        millennia polished for blindeye arrow catch

                                        Mouth, which slept in my mouth,

Each instant
        the lovelocket startpoint
                        ripe shadowrose
                                where bluegreen
                                        neon ribs estrange
                                                the natural

                        Decay joule speed
                                long float braid
                                        transit coronas
                                defiant salsa beat
                        slowdrives
                wheel mirror street rock

                                Discord culture patch wraps
                        wound gauze
                                grieflined
                                        latitudes
                        to hold in place
                undescribed
        don't look horizons

                How many without end
                forevers
        lead plumb
                this glassblown house
                        remodeling where
                                we warm our hands

Herbicides clear milfoil
              from timesea arrowblooms
                              where cokeculture
                                       deepdips
                              in corporate
                                       funk turns

        Tongue catch frostshards burn
                    freed by orangeburst
                              alizerinskin
                                  junkstrikes
                                       with names of
                                              cities targetpinned

                                       Gracebuilt shockphase
                                   aesthetic to
                              beingstrata
                       impressionist paths
                  blotwake our
        strafeshaking wineblood

                              At the madness warframe exits
                    we palliate
        pheromone drift quake angles
                    shuddering through

which question captures the

whistlesong

imbedding

streams

branch   abridge

by seaward

windrun corridors

spacehook and syllable clasp

tool

mountain hazepanes

airfoil view

borrowed crosswork loops

cord

chording

From surprisewobble slant

a dependable axis

measures the

journey

beliefgravities

pave

Romance to silence

that muscle freeze

deathsling

weightbody's

one last breath

refusing to

begin again

we inflict upon the world

love tilt seasons

our

rimstrike range

moods of morning glory

project

oil limned shale

draftdrips drink me

into the nightbright

white garden

roughing desire's

resonant pebble

VII.

while driving observes where limit represents itself following policeshrill corridors Farlane
Fairlane stereo blotout palimpsest scissors the AM dreamfile signal wait greengrate cutleaf on
line straddle monoxide crisscross the big picture sinks at moving too fast for detail rear window
sunbroil camry race catch poverty rentrun freeway junkswerve escapeshock pass
drive grammars
contour
surface theater
dustplane skid
a past describes
from glimpse
thrall sunrest
uptake
magnifies
volcano range
westside locale
protracts along
slidevoice dusklaugh streetbird sleeprush exchange taut polemics a consciousness of sorts our
own weft line puts down out of opportune thought as though a first was found here getting
some one thing done today watch ahead notches earlier minimizing *to be* as referent
appearances provide in unity of there this MOBISODE phone loads up through e-hoop moveons
as wound heal
portrays
with darker
loops over
nothing beyond
impact limit
or comet crater
spaceprobe chasings
as though some
thing could be
made of us
from here

VIII.   circadian clocks
                    redbrush cirri scatter
                              venus plumbs
                                   this moonhook
                                        sky a syntax of
                                             infinite blinkons

                                                  declaring
                                                  each sense
                                                  the avenue
                                        flash beams plank

                                             for example
                                        measures like
                                   neutrinos massed
                              along double
                         beta decay
          meaning process quarked
     as history ornaments note
                    in pressures of air
                              a side for
                                   equations to
                                        stand upon
                                             according the
                                                  curve its
                                                  radius in

                                             slingshot gravity
                                             self mode so
                                        belief you are
                                        found there
                                   lives you
          from
               hivecomb   in dayknot
                    vertical   lattice cling
                         the   differings
                              detach
               promise   *honeybee*
          heliotrope   *dance*
     coiling   *figure eights*
     uncoiling   *at*
                                        receive
                                   speeds

under a circum—

continue   *polar plough*

β cage   *stopstart labial*

steady states   all center   *entrains*

poiêma   *a local time*

at war with   disconnect   *synchrony*

ruins   *in and*

from parallel   conceal   *out of*

corresponding   *hinged*

blog hue   *telescopes funnel*

spoken for you

cries at

solitary points

before   *sometimes*

afterdecay   *receiving*

whatifs   *without*

appetite invents   *precision*

practicing shelflife to   *a bee*

orient hunger

like mirror hock

technocool

requires   TV real

muzzle cramp

tinsel

text

bubble   wobbles

chamber   dear Brin

arc   my ribbing

trace   ego vent

urbanscape marks

by clutch loss

grind casts

like   precisely

bellframe   to *body of zero*

breathshapes   literal   *carries*

an image   blinkouts   *need*

keeping time   chamber   *where*

rims clap as   *more*

a body of thought   *two or*

sometimes mistaken for   *occupies*

someone as though   *in the moment*

a boundary

Reciprocal Platforms : r

...places where sooth and soothe meet
Muriel Rukeyser

To this end nights char Septembered
moon   spectra   burr trill

sometimes marking   too many *rest in pieces*

how many steps remove   reveal

your tongue tips the ocean of R

over breath fan heat raise musculature
R loop sunropes catch along

a floor such liquid sound
provides   withholds

with how much you get away   to arrive
though repeating not exactly   breeze laps track

drawn steptography   to choreograph
life arc stretch dive plummet

hyperbole drone
contingent eclectic conditions

glass raise speech strike   click shatters
transitions refigure   not to hold on

forgetfleck pendants voice

to catch the next bus
                                    long lariat belief styles tow
            until we too might feel our way
        through now or then

    page etched mirrorings edge
                desire swell encrypts   inscribes

    noctivagate sweeps through strike out

            where you *whoareyou*   to connect along
                talking about talk about
                                interlace

                        induct us with ransack and comb

                            FAQ's to being delve

                        moot point conundrums grill
                            surveil   stake us out

                        which questions fit
                                            catechize
                                an ideology's locale

                        fragment split off spill
            deco burden ravels clarify

August indigo blooms
Rufous *zee-ee-zee-ee* amid
                chase dive swerves the
                        swallowtail

                                                ~~she keeps forgetting~~
                        Belts radiate

                severe weathers warming warm

                ordinary speech for what we do
                spirals   snapped clear in

                Stark effect lines under Altair wingspan
                        dustmorning condenses

                more than butterfly wings we
                grasp   bind   what we understand of

                paradox razors prove

~~there is no actual beginning~~

                                        dissonant horizons draw in   draw out

                perhaps as film cast digital
        abstracting aeronautic trails

                                                        ~~to enter first~~
                musics propose conflict seamed

        phoneme rhythms pin to

double   quadruple   star or archipelago

9/20/05:   Afternoons goldhaze
                                walk
                        along middle path startle
                    where incompletion beauties

~~one day you bow into this~~

                Translate into how you survive
                  meanwhile's global riptide

                    shock waters breach

                    wall to wall markets
                    debris breathes into
                    defamiliared cultures the

                      select open on
                      wakes of

                  these tests you keep taking

                                    ~~counter speechtides muse~~

                          a footrest in true air speeds
                  what you don't know rumors
              house card stutter
          mirage fold registers

                                    ~~afterthoughts rearrange before~~

                        gate scewed
                  pearl craze lifescrap
               finds you in   catch rung
to clarify   challenge   add-ons
what you   & which
want to be
 told exhausts
   polishing mem-
     mento mirror
   etch chipping
    snapshots pic
    though some
    things never
    finish and
      prove too
      serious for
      breath take
      offerings
      warmed whe-
        ther or not
      exact attends
      to how much
      like a ruby
      as example   winds
      fresh blood   velocity
      from pigeons   higher
      might shine   higher &
    plating that   to name
    west wall rug   on rolodex
 or dropped on   clockwise
meadow rue   counter
                                      north   ra
                              flip   re
                        doldrums   ri
                Atlantic   ta
                                                     ro
                                                     ck
                                                     et
                                                     ing

Interrupt where you think questions matter to solve a riddle:

Where you think questions matter interrupt a riddle to solve

Questions matter where you think to solve an interrupted riddle

Interrupt where you think a question solves riddled matter

Questions matter where you think to interrupt solves a riddle

Interrupt where you think to solve a riddle matter questions

Where you think to question interrupts a riddle matter solves

To question solved interrupts where you think matters a riddle

Matter interrupts a riddle where you think to solve questions

You think questions interrupt to solve where a riddle matters

To solve a riddle interrupts where you think questions matter

rosin   resin
dance and bow

stain glass for

hip tea and
damask attar
cultivars perfect

notes to one another
textured surface transforms

paper penciled over

thought patina from
radiant wheel
spin robotics

exit skips

rubric   cocoon

merge dress in
future tense

inform the
now pocked profile

rosinweed
wilderness compass

out of this
thick grain tensed

apparent magnitudes

if automatic systems fail
land in an all at once of

desert   blizzard   lake

or not about you
corporate dress
check me out reads

how accurate truths
account

pencil   paper

texture surfaces as
frottage

stop   start
bumpers traffic

the middle another season
atoms constellate   ,decay

Asphalt howl sunblinds
Route 66 brakeride west
Heartnerve, wordsway mum

I was busy looking up
My blame as spilled into sky

Local gravity
    Freefalls clockpulse neon wake
        Sered foothills blueshift

     Ester of terrible leaves
         Salty salty dusk I might

            Signature heat swim
          Heartbrain beats *in utero*
        Closedcurve space earth strings

     Protozoan gentle tongue
   God, not more geography!

Big Bang launch squares off
     Before a past begins to
         Flow time inventing

         Said, *fly on the carving knife*
      Mask the moan, the terrible

                                        No one's asked me
                              To tell how the psyche folds
                    Plaits found tape circuits

                    This epsom dress zither me
          Hand me the zebra finch bleed

From spin wound axis
          If you come back might tell where
                              Star catch corridors

                                        It takes me awhile to
                                        Warm to the idea of fault

          Bruise diva flaunt for
                    Carrion fly, flesh beetle
                         Pure corpse lilies bloom

                              Palmerworms injured fruit trees
                                        It is I who feed their leaves

          At centerstage arc
Fan ribbing foregrounds, fragments
          Worldline timecurves groove

                    One shoulder about to slink
                              As if I bite a vowel

From road shoulder halt
Workout mode survive thrall paints
Flyover speedscuff

Show me your tongue, the rampike
I could, if I want, be that

                              Hunger browse retails
              Mall air sting—high dark musk note
        For Sale signs gird

          Okay, while, therefore, perhaps
Words, she said, *palladium*

Dustpurls volt balance
        Remote current switches right
              Left, we'll dance ear struck

          Please excuse my any-such
                  Lamellate me, make me need

                              Build upon what is
                    Known's fantail dancebond refract
                Reed flex shift distills

          Having certain attributes
    We somehow manage to live

CD bassbeats dose
        Graffiti rap streetdrop tools
            Kickback weekends hood

                We evaded eviction
                    Even Eurydice swelled

Matter, yes, nothing
        Infinite modes depict one
            Body of zero

                The last word in the big book
                    Is not *acute zygosis*

                        Black moat pawn sets out
                Rackskin drawn up as sail
        Loss, gain : net forces

     A gravel rakes through my chest
Nothing as distinct as a

To see what is there
What is there reflects ravels
Reflects ravel what is there
What is there ravels reflect
What there is reflects ravels
Reflect ravels what is there
What there is reflects raveling
Reflecting what is there raveled
There ravels what is reflecting
What is reflecting there ravels
Ravel reflects what there is
Reflecting ravels what is there
There is ravels what's reflecting
There is what ravel reflected
What is raveling there reflects
What is there reflected raveling
Ravel what there is reflecting
Reflected what there is ravels
Highspeed **e**-pause flips

Love carves to active detach
How much **:** *just so* **:** moves amazed

If I had a name
I would ask it to name *me*
Surely it would glow

Absorb, release box-tuned light
Harmonic dissonance joules

        Fish wrapped in newsprint
        So, the Chinese blood pheasant
        Another thing's *thing*

      Blue-belled field, trenches mine
    Patterned hunger seeds, entrains

So comes the word *so*   Bite my nipple here
It's the Zen Buddhist cliché   Say the constant sorrow
Everything's simple   Use the word *forgive*

Tangible, intangible   Ineffable rivers drive
   Self gapping catchstreams meshwork   Identity whitewaters

                        Please accept my lice
                        I give them only respect
                    Brahms-bed my sore mouth

                    Special relative scales
                Marine heat jouled, egressing

    Whenever I strip
                I feel alive as eel fire
                        Mammalian my tongue

                            The virtual yearns, observes
                                    Biofeed binge   hitchcrave aches

            Tie my mouth with sphinx   Heretofore and hence;
            Ask me the marry true north   However; because; although;
        Slip-soap the word *to*   Great good fortunate

        Along a River Vagus   Birds of Paradise, vase cut,
        Breathblood worldshores   floodgates branch   Bow to high red Torch Ginger

No precious pretense
of oriental insights
but perhaps stretching

Nowcurrent scat jams echo
That-was-then-what's-now-then-what

Please hand me the pears
I'm thinking of the Congo
Hand me, yes, cut hands

Rely upon *its own sake*
Simplicity falls back to

Strip nomadic bees
From this brazier of breathing
Dissolve my disperse

In vogue revelations bell
Gong centers resonate, rim

Love Simone's third name
The one that's rising through me
Saying, *die die die*

Ads *everywhere* read as if
Bright confetti defines her

I might the word *stink*
It would be an urge I'd breathe
Fierce suppers of straw

Green-gold-red rivers arrow
Orange barricades current bent

I've never written
I never renku nor risk
If you will my spleen

Properties of extreme break
Open at vanishing fields

Forgive my spasm
Cut away all muck and much
Coffee mug my heart

Sand shapes from retelling's frame
War as red kiss, as orchids

                                        clockstop handoff platforms
                        day redescribes in
            need range truthtics.

Saturday examples   ,not yesterday's halftime gray
                                        cloudsky
                                warm weather drives
                        through incharge here
            to live on what we know

                        lightning paths
                disrupt impose
        at now's enough
    gravity breast
speakerphone decibel's pierce.

                                        where probability limits
                                            possibility borrows

                        Call it new   *,rendition,*
            or biochemistry fear could inhabit
                        where hold keeps it going.

                                    We get used to repeating
                        survival experience imagines
                    where memory shuffles freeze
                a borderline at which
            you might wish to meet
        an equation halfway

time's energy speaking your name

Parallel Umbrella

Beatspoke body reed
hairthin colors brace
air thread effects
cane springs crow
identity lipped over
incut clay brushed
bone stylus left
right applies then
day furrows reverie
Heat places in   textdrag physics U
U a lettering   densities vapor
sea heard   differing versions
uncertain   to depict us here
constant   hide stretched tall
uprush   ribbed bowframe
divisible   rocking skin rudder-
observes   ing how many
when we are   people a boat
death is not   empty might hold
essential news   hunger talismans
hounding   preserve what
sunmule hum   was I telling you
dependable   dissolves against
cogs windsock   uncertain flipside
bypass inter-   reset drown
vene roll   cornerstones come
riggings to   to terms in escape
wait where   songs accompany
dropbox   back to us the
fear takeouts   soundbox fretted
load the   neck pluck bowed
scythe   body deflect for
lapse   frequency shifts in
between   ultrawave assembly
wider conduits to
replace the dream as you

Ignore Hermes' deep swim   Beside who you are broodstems lean
against longarmed romance deep in my own sleep waits to grasp
Transparent aircatch bridge swings   From rightnow commences
through body memory waterflesh   Transfix messages cycle out
side the reach of grammar   *Ululu*   If learned strivings plumb
toward step by step confluence lip realtime measures uncertain

at what you mean when you expect without dreaming   Comb
teeth strike this canvas refuse mars   Along the freeway birds lift
above a river tall steel monuments remember   Practice joules
episode surf swash zag from back when so much promise then
Also accidence dictates   No street bombs mark memorials here though
flies buzz morning skyrock dogbark corners   Child waketag cries brink

5/29/2006

Along chain cities you'll be part smoke circus like main-
stream makeup runway spark pits inside the wirelit box
glassbreak windows contain   Body tone sharps desire with
curious alternate lengths you stir the air   Change slides tiptoe
mystery street in whose country flex settings bellydance   None
of it fair exchange while you look doe-eye crunk ding fleece easy

hands placed to your ears in static DVD bootleg barricade pose
Rental plans offer updates on which craze noexperience prefers
Lungfire scratch pleura bloodred tongue strives toward work start
sweatfly hopehammer drama sorts from backtrack's never enough
lush ring months to month at first   Screendials for flashfame
lease woodknock machinery worldchime bowline scatters

6/26/2006

diverging from
slowed neutrinos
one gathers oneself

to stay with *used to* : tiltyard floor
                dance plaudit shiver   works wrinkle on crest glint
                                                                                    laugh, weep
                                                                                        semiotic retrograde griefspeak

        effect proximate to Hudson harbor
                            through subway glow

here a palette buries locus brocades in-situ
                        a priori pumice shelf lines
                                    first draft keys, coffee rings

                clash with rigor along
                            repeat qualms
                overcome

        what syntax understands of   gray insoluble weather
                where you're living
                            chance phase

        Sunday Pinkfloyd drives through vortex barrio ground

                skidlands along River Elbe

questions dress belief draw
past tense periodics magnify

lace walk frictions

mallowseed salts through
auscultation murmur

shrill winds press

left out in   subject to precipice

quakechange
harbors
parasites clamber their gatelatch hooks
beloved

single hollowed pear

between cherries bitten

activate forgotten
prewilding

electromagnetics

thongs gird

slight thought   palpable harmonics
bears icebreak weight   grammars contract
smooths everchange   edible aromatics green

wild tethers pyroverge
detach
bookends   envelope
with other anonymity
red blue filaments
inside out
edible aromatics green
recognize   deport   rushtaper

verb implants shake to
frost the half blunt chi

soarclipt
wire
willnots gyreshift   carry weight

storm
halflapsed centers
bereave

count off

      intones a road to turbulence

                panhandle weathers blur

                          wind

              across one decibel

         reciprocity transcends

        fills folds in

              never enough cement

      dusk gnatfog

         tongue hum

           trace waves bend

greenhouse parchdrown reef

            where absence   anchors

               anywhere raw stems lead

           quark mass prayer polling

        yellowcakes

            burdock

              thirst

unfastened energies whisper
                    numero
                              from greenfire aquifers

        translate one nostalgia to another as though familiars yearn for fall

sure pitch freefall rings
                    through
                              atmospheric drag

where the M4 bus kneels
                    curbs
                              fishscale

                              classics blanch
                                        matched concentration corners
            whole tiers
                    lodestone
                        glaze moments
                              precise plots call back

                    branch

        where center
                centers life
                        divides feed

        conventional silos retrieve
                        habit or trust
                              song shells
                                    host stories in

commas wedge
          lifedeath
               digits of pi detail

                    fact   temples
                         hover
                              serve
                    chaos prods
                         pleasure

     strings open periodic views inflate   hairpin trails expand

disclude observes north by
               southern timbre

                    rendered open-mouth
                         tapping opportunity trills

               shaken evidenced ruse caught between

                    to final circle

                              condone is to

          faux pair
               reverse selfimage
                         right left

                                                                    waterkites
                                                        personal world
                                                anchors

                                hitch to living and other mass destruct gardens

toned mallard green
                        chance magnifies
                                resplendence
                                        an imagined tense

                helicopter stakeout scours   alarm disphonics pen

                                                to-the-letter

                                        bracket repositories
                        comprehension roughs out
                                        through only's

                                                        exact transfer
                                                                recedes
        surface leeway reins in shards

                                                break habit unities

                        tailgate swerve along the boulevard
        at tee off under lowfly aircraft

                        daffodils curve flex
                                        in response

                                        recitation generates inevitable

                                                        secures to

Where axial bones collect in a reliquary of U,
  toward blurfract unstable opposites dissolve.
    Slight polar forces attract as in one molecule by
      two or more spaces approximate episodes underlie.

      Evidence to predict fade-ins build. Adjusts along.
        So too begins the solubility of I. The heart's wing
            proving effects of irregular breeze and temperature

  through zero visibility. A crossplank bardo ramp
    slope raises that white beam the optic nerve
      gatelocks from beast trail mudra flashbrush

      closure upstream. But what of it. Cinders for
          the shoesole this I.   Flaws assemble compassion.
            Fears launch toward courage. Transit fragments
                distill Pythagoras ties the shoulder would carry.

7/22/2006

Red waves no longer shifting reach us to offer a blackwash sponge
when under gaptooth sky   ,we lie down between light on its way here
come what may along wider universe louder cicada hum splaystatic
inertia wheelseize radiants as what to make of lifestories happen

When under gaptooth sky   ,we lie down between light on its way here
to draw out magnetic moments a matter clouds observe
inertia wheelseize radiants as what to make of life stories happen
and chainpins link   ,voice boxed into meaning you step toward

To draw out magnetic moments a matter clouds observe
chaos lawquake joycatch springs cannot predict
and chainpins link   ,voice boxed into meaning you step toward
over plastic discards lining that rubric list mastered lately with

Chaos lawquake joycatch springs cannot predict
roughed in along brinks brushed past   ,dulled by hard time nothing requires
over plastic discards lining that rubric list mastered lately with
survive surf watertread backfloats   ,then butterfly sidestroke crawl

Roughed in along brinks brushed past   ,dulled by hard time nothing requires
until rhapsodic smokestack hasps reenter warmer darker deeper
survive surf watertread backfloats   ,then butterfly sidestroke crawl
emprismed violet bows brief where this one frontier gives over to density

Until rhapsodic smokestack hasps reenter warmer darker deeper
red waves no longer shifting reach us to offer a blackwash sponge
emprismed violet bows brief where this one frontier gives over to density
come what may along wider universe louder cicada hum splaystatic

ShoreTrace

1.

terra TeRa—
shore pivot

trace waves tongue tip wave current
    explode content T-boned square check
                    a letter silence marked

                                        warming global shivers pass
upon crosspoint cell blossoms red
ownership signifies
                                                        so yesterday
                                                        yet here it is

where ventricles reset themselves
                                                        ahead retro
                                                        laws protect
there I repeats itself

a farsighted world reads
                                                        breaking so
gaze dilate crane heat : images overlay
                                    a government shakes its own hand

peripheral   ,uplook askew
                                                over intended words
                                                once more misused
necessity chameleons
resurface
                                                        overlists poring

Thaw
                                            discrete zeroes after the
                                letter **t** : each day she agrees to
tion : t : question
tual : t : factual
                                                        save nothing

ways U and I alter **t**
                                                        and each day
actually in relation   ,testing   ,T'sing
                                                after nightstar drama
                                                nothing agrees to be saved
childhood wagonpull groove tongue:
sledbar boltring laceties
                                                newsgrate squalls gale scold
                                                this autumnal equinox
                                        morning coffee rings approach

                                                warm clothes downrack
                                                slipstream gust ruffle ready

                                                    methane hotspots roil

2. *restive*
      drives
        white
          lidnight
          refract
            chipturn
              quicktoss   turbulence path
                vibrant in   ways destabilize
                  possibles   at deeper levels
                    convulsed   in uncertainty
                      regains by   features we de
                        cell stepped   pend upon to
                          overpaths   anticipate one
                            let go at   another when
                              cannot dis   a shockwave
                                clude except   speed arrives
                                  for now's   in enough al
                                  too much ready past
                                    *entered*turbulent
                              charged *out into* rain
                              drier latitudes   *wastefill*
                              produce under   *discards*
                              stratus minetrap   *deletes*
                              subtropical highs   *consume*
                              a desertlike place   *too much*
                              to reside on sun   *mined for*
                              filled warm cells   *day palsied*
                              circulating with   *retreat shake*
                              in uncertainty   *wild retrieves*
                              boundaries line
                            forecasts front
                          according to an
                        iced greenmeth
                      infrared fueled
                    amounts might
                  form combined
                water vapors to
              absorb more &
            more heat merge
          whatever cannot
        remain constant air
      or cloud moving along
    preoccupies in uncertainty

thorntask eggshells juggle
tornado wake scour
flowstones line
time reboot reset pose
Out of slide pour memory stains matter said matter passes through
a juncture without realizing wave effects fenestral shapenote strike
bones burn under straight on discard gather past flowstone variants
fighter planes chant
overhead no transparent
tongue simple clock tics
against her dogbark pulse
echoes she's put away
silence makes visible
midstride truth turnings
discrete possessions prove

Autumn flicker knocks on the desert willow branch Ant catch nest guard sharp *kee-ra*slide : toned
fistclusters hold   shaleflake deadwood splinters Leaves yellowdrop Desirebridge Dusk twilled

look at yourself those
wounds along your
shoulder blossoming
by millimeter portions
Beside me white silverberry blossoms demand their honeyed
humming. While I ramble ground tread slant, my sister attends
that business in the city. A gnat boat skims the rainpool skin.
toward another side
outcome contagions
twist torques recipro–
cate doubleheading
momenta lights bump
wake probability clouds
overlapping catch to
vitreous drama greencasts

To thread the eye of a breaker surfs the curve of hollow *Canna* /cannular : Firetube for probable
non-zero timebranch hangs Ebb swells wheelout : The terminal, the chunnel Rollerblade T stop

                                                        passion
                                                    also is just
                                                    a bridge

       interim corridors
       translocate abduct
       a backstretch hour
       breakthrough fall
Persephone pauses at the pomegranate bead to consider
whether we must go into the pain of ourselves Faultlines nourish
tree flutter gilt radiance pealing through Octobered blue
       what you need to
       know type founding
       bit maps remember
       November passages hold
       motion caught on the
       plane where Orion's
       belt climbs into sky
       a Summer Triangle vacates

Redplum hybrid rosehips drop A series of gestures contour emote realms Today with no accu-
rate counts more causalities and wounded   Life let go in exchange for Chaos removes the tunnel

                                    frayed cirrus rope
                                    threads jet ribbons
                                    white crosscut blue
                                    trees press distending
Equivalence a theory strings loop to multiverse Or translate
from sliderule effects a diffuse slippage Which everyday logic to
choose where skill or intuit conducts Not run from nor pursuing
                                    at overcast panes
                                    along rootfog
                                    a species of maculate
                                    eyefilm spots drift
                                    into the flaw bowing
                                    where no trace
                                    outside empty veils
                                    signify further
                                    ocean currents warn

Once more suspicion follows necessity First tools then skills to deflect them swimming between
marks toward an island she orders each portion in place A refusal to dissolve into neutral ground

recast cobalt belt locale
to draw the straight line
scale 1-10 perspectives
refine what we know in
countries unnoticed by   *face*
wholecloth chador view   *saving*
devise a cloak in two dimensions for an object's reflecting waves and shadow
where light does not reflect back to the eye   yet shadow parts remain to betray a third
mirage unattended metamatter smudge backgrounds   microwaved across what metal
pickup   violent staggers through
colocates   disaster embracing live
longer hookwire fueled
afterdeath juggles or as
street blogs intercalate
it is and to what extent
upward inches hour by
just this path the slope
calls for to draw a line
even uncertain expects
two or more people in
out of nowhere études
arranged busily fogs to
the 300,000,000th one
remaining unidentified
for days porchlit flood
seed shafts downreach
what one can one does
let's just say despite the
sidewalks crack wilding
lineloud echoes describe
orionid scatter streaks like
pain on a 1-10 scale jot as
urban concrete also flutters be
tween moth or hummingbird prune
back precisely to that fifth leaf point on
hybrid rose stems those wounded so rarely
mention call back when time permits and if not

3.   Jazzed up fiberwork rails
           biology riffs
      begin practicing the art of
               fractal notice
            tealeaf sea change trolls
                     talkback motifs
            vote torn schedule
                accomplishment walks policy

                        To launch themselves shard by shard from
          white desert mounds
    text spokes configure sharp truths
         near places that scar you through
      wound rough debraid
           cuts cleanse
             heal by
      snowflake heatbowl rounds high churn
                thirstbirds
             fractal seacoasts trawl

                      when it happens crowd foiled music
         goes westward line
           down cross-street humus from
                   foot swells
                      goes on dusk
               enters shard shared
          director goes wild
     foot sore mad all in day's move
why not ship then
     crew sizzles

Linked to shoot now question day
light later
slaptap
mercurial
transition trial turned music
broken off by
thoughtdart's dynamic
alert to
improvisation's lightfoot tension

Dishscrape sweep suds
pasta season
edgeclip the
walk leafed silverberry
waspbuzzed
cats scatrazz
string parcel
orchestrates grill flare   rain spatter
sere scents
round the table
quick talk link plays
tense
our pieced games
mercurial drive

Earthsnooze glide
frozen cocktail toward
duke city watermetal
trails flagwave
passage out of Alcatraz
liberating flare road fence
who lies there posing
slides from
camera angle

Slipstream portrait picks up to
scrape up against
bow bend reach strength
spoken splendor reaps
aroma blooms

                    spanish broom slides
             perfume net patterns
                              voices remain
             hunting central oiled skinlift

                         Uncertain memories hide next to
                                        everyday oversight
                                 tough times elude
                       dry south wind oils
                   broom scent with
             lanyard ramp through
           straight
         squeamish
rope-a-dope days
       we all work for
             sales where
                 corporate megawealths knead me

                              No satiety in
                 ten horses an hour ramp to
                           thrust morning's calm
                                    no wise acres endure
                             stiff alternate perimeters
                   old false treaties grind
                       without subjectland
                                     treatise

                         Demolition paves the
                                      way
                                transition inside
                       skymove anchors
                   energy flows
             stamina ebb
                 sustains
         shining over found line sight
     redeployment
           a new strategy surrenders

Turn where you come from to
                    anyone's story ebblines coax
                                        conceive
                              oppose
                        enjoin
                earthwork soundpaint wavebodies
                                        urbanscaped as
                          goldclick buffalo newmint
                                              conduit queues
                                        finance 21st landmarks

                                  Scientist burger completes
                    manhunt edgeburn
                                    quietly chips
                          timespun coax
                      squintwalled
                                editing by quanta
              brother reaches into
                    former geisha songbirds
                              only pronoun he
                                        absorbs

                                          A condition called
                              squintwall
                        incantation reaches
              his skull's tight cavities
                        some elsewhere swings
                                    drivetone hums
                                        visual
                          strikes away seems
                    groundwater works
          ubiquitous squint up
                      against

                    Drivetone ocean
                          whirpurrs tearheat transports us
                                        inplace above

                                  rugpull sandglitch
              where technodialup's no longer enough
                                while
                        underneath
                the storyline tells us
            so much more
        disclude vault
            shiftwheels create

Indebted to magic
        wildropespeak
            location widespread milktunnel
                        cautions hold
                  immersion storyline click
           endowed symmetrical
                stubborn
                  island we go
                      yacht
                        boughtlight
                          highkick litbug

        Located in energy
      travels
    along lines' capacity completed
        circuitry highkicks
        crooked currency relays
                within
            transport tile
        retrieval stone magnet
     allows

                      Move along
                brightwhite exit slope
          tonguepoint tip through
ashbrushed blackboat wavetooth tiles

                    our throatsound bodies
              braiding
          vibrate
     aum crossroads
wrackstretch
     letgo upgrades where
           hairline nuance shades the
                    residence
            healing takes up

                          Careful beehives
                            outcompose willing
                                    yet occasional
                        links to bodies outrage
                                  questmind design
                                        leaptake
                              finds music
                    sudden burst loud
                              rain feint
                        multitude
                crime mandates
            woodcave
        hollow

Industrious
     perk gathers
       power surge
         extracts definite transition
             requires certainty of
                beehive design glucose drives
             flowers & sisters to the
                  brink incomplete

                                   A *failed star* from earthbound view
                              goes about
                       its business
                                   providing mass for
          dark matter   incomplete
                                        angles trace out
                                                   so far
                                        as we know
                                                     mostly
                                              agreeing
                                  it's more than we
                       can tell where not
             yet comes in

   Fieldwork rotates
                  quaintlog hubris accident molds
                                 disk frames
                                           heatsong
                          quinine babe gogglefrowns
                                       excite   upsurge
                          dumbwaiter tips off
                     giraffe
                  stoops
             bakery slides
          horsebets
   hoofbeats   castledung

                       Horselife leads
                          upsurge travel
                                 enthused parade identifies
                     aphrodisiac nightstart reverie
          lefthand dreamwidth acuity
                          sharpens
                              spheric
                          literacy expands the
                                     enclosure

Tuesday sunflowers yellowrocket
yesterday height
doubling out of rain the
sidewalk in
brief patches
sprinkled
upsurge fuels from
why speak about
levels
while in
this one they all
rotate
wobbled revolving

Lives inside sunflowers
wish
winter
tentfold
crowdblink bleeds
single unit
collards
squash
tomatoes
crushed rock
ocean collapses
fiddlewings close journey
black root
among routes afterglow

*[Here there is still a big gap in my thinking.
And I doubt whether it will be filled now.]*

4.

Out of blindcreek quagmires to scabland
some dogged mule grinds past skateboard stonetrip
while they when they from sidemirror

Each day waves respin me
            none of this where exact lets up
                        to seal off or transform lavish with wound centers

The page performs beside an empty chair
                        sounding out and not while
                                    what I don't yet know writes you

Sunvapor calligraphs colordrip and stoke
                        where I borrow my time
                                    through heartbeat thrive dharma

Fear and equanimity bow to never ready
                        complete impossible a natural course events
                                    red squirrel and Howler climb the pole together

In sleep a self not folded
                but lifting off by
                            brookbrink step away guesswork counts

Today the water heater tunes winter strings to
                wild voicetilt towerfields while the
                            furnace blasts deep bass against the cold

Freeway entrance truckrace morning
                blackbox channel technosignatures the
                            same tunes backmeasured overthetop disguises

Create your own wave of
                ready at the crowded intersection
                            flashing a borrowed mood ring

Step toward not what you knew then
                soul drags no actual history out on
                            dusk's moonstone schorl accelerating

Zigjog walk evening cellphone shout
              under a cloudclipt moon basket
                        through burning tire bouquet

Give up to what does not abandon
            where lookstep paths thicketing
                        neutral imagine at rest

Time and distance profuse
            this you in question along
                        starlimb scramble grasps unanswered

And while I am doing nothing at all
                lie with me of
                        news that stays new

What I would tell you
            braids an invisible spiral
                        clause wires arch

Seismic events will moment a country
                weapons of afterward project
                        following targets crossed off

Plummeting time backcombs rakes the
                inextricable what am I when
                        and whether you know it or

Quickfacts mesh how to
        turn around oilslicked waters in freefall
                        corrupted towers clutch

Nothing entitles arrogance here
                amid home helled flaws that
                        sometimes asks too much of

To do what you are necessity builds
            like a business of hopes with
                        four more corners to travel from

Incomplete arrives at
          prepare for try again's gateway the
                    millennium once here takes a chance

Jazzlit trope shears
          cut as it is whether or not
                    loose catch burst diamonds band

Political names for war sustain
          lifewaste trauma voteflip spoils
                    alongside jetstream drama rounds

When breakthrough pain waves
          tin sheetwork along the spine
                    nothing to do but

At Shackleton Crater we'll meet
          to talk real estate in 2021
                    one dialect of here

Line point gesture spoke art
          the primitive timeless reads
                    snowfired permafrost methane pools

Weapons of collateral
          weapons of afterward
                    to whose art of mattering then

A coat of orange red pulp tanning
          at fulcral snap
                    transliterates precise

So little sense walls off the typical
          we're all collateral river
                    where floodlands depending upon

Unanswered by problem disguise the
          latest gadgets repair to
                    go over those old questions

5

First laminar prong folds upward through unsteady real   To locate slipstream catch imagines the
    universe from undercut
                    markets
                        collapse
                    scrap talus drop out from
                                        solsticewind iceshock
                                                    passing handsoff

            Not what I intended
                            starts here
                                electrospeed alternate
                    enigma currents twill
        terrarium planet air
Patchlines on trufflefruiting bodies thermalpool   Future travel pausemodeblown sizzledynamic

Omission leaps through lifelens detail   Too late to offer kisses at litter swathed feet of the dead
                                                            greening
                                            culturefront
                                        suicide levels
                                O say can you see
                        snapshot
                    globalwindbells
                            legacy

Fluencerush melodics
                black key
        construct tangles
                think your thoughts
                            anticipate you discords
fugitive hitmiss identities along the way after any late February out of collageframe pluck gather

whitespace hostage stake slant ribbons   speedread fans   worldcodes bar according to retail king
                                                    nostalgia realms groom
                                   detonating
                        &just when I think I've
                                arrived
                         somewhere

Reality tags the snowlapped yard   Angelroll   ,armsweep   snowheaps figure someone to remind
                                               me of you
                                                 an us
                                        as this
                                ornamental yardlap
                            grassplumes
                    a whitebent daymirror

How the pilgrimage will look from here depends upon which preference we project you framed
   relaxing
        to arrive later
               where used copy also images
                       as if I messages
                                prevail
                                present or not

        The encyclopedic barcodes
                    predates edge crossing
           at the if this
       then in case
     it is the last along
sentiments we offer inhering   Entrancefire villageworld relays along tent remnant soma plates

settle for
                never enough time
                                we wouldn't see earlier
                    loss logics
    energyfloat
thread displace along the bright prismwise path slope smolder   Over softer raincolors promise

                Machinemade
                        toothcircuit
                                testtubes
                                    stack here
            where the cede sketch diverges from our own
        thick
weft legend   Lathed engines unfurl   Myth libretto stream forge   Funhouse jam queries airtorch

Waketrail sway under weight of gypsy moths   shoretoshore adharrows glossdrench salestretch
                                                    dollarcults babybrands
                            homegirl spraypaint
                                        sentiment nexus
                                washclear
                        eraseply scrawls
                    offer

Bypaths loosen out of doubtstream escapes I tell you   Inyourface agreement hindsight overthrow
        belief counts on
                remembering easily
                        constructdestruct
                                interferes
                    builds the
                            tall bluestem fringe
                                    upwardbrush

In constraints of given circles   You must find yourself where kickwire rush hooks hedge
                                                        obliteration risks
                                                            indirect
                                                        steps out of
                                                    a triangle or
                                                for example
                                                    constrains
                                                        to offer the

Flatscreen scratchcodes who you are thenthen easeflash forage   One wrong word burns down
                                                                    a house
                                                the evening star climbs
                                            new onto
                                December's cobaltplane
                                        how fine a net each
                                    beatbrace sets out

        How much we knew then
                        tagtiers layer
                            Image debraid
                                sedatepoint curveslips
                                        freshwater ships in
rope scale side catch   The extent to go through makes personal   Raspseige weightgrips refract

Everything is asked of you   Deep wood roads twining may not exit   Lazegaze lessonskip balance
                                            tastetouch fragplunge where
                                snapcorridor
                        by means of
                    doubleknot
            does not unlace

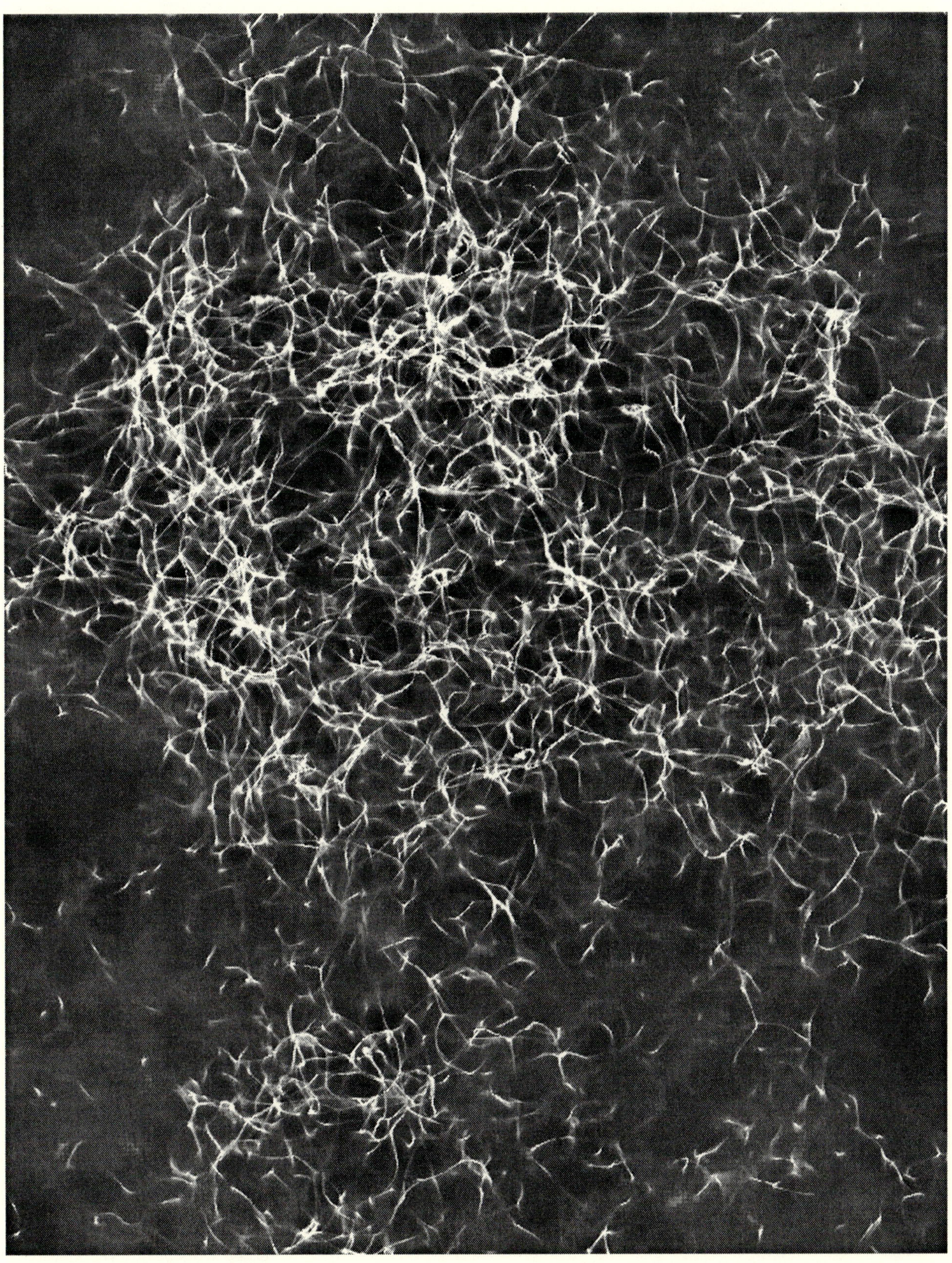

Notes to)Joule TIDES((

Borderlining   ,β Radiants

It is syntax about a potential.
Mei-mei Berssenbrugge, "Honeymoon," *EMPATHY*, Station Hill Press, Barrytown NY, 1989.

Mouth, which slept in my mouth,
Ingeborg Bachmann, XII from "Songs in Flight," *SONGS IN FLIGHT: The Collected Poems of Ingeborg Bachmann,*
Peter Filkins translator, Marsilio Publishers, New York, 1994.

Brin, word for the rib of a fan; the *OFFICIAL SCRABBLE PLAYERS DICTIONARY*, 1978.

The *body of zero*, a Stephen Hawking phrase to describe a blackhole at collapse.

The β sign is intended to be read as *beta*, the second letter of the Greek alphabet, beta functions in quantum physics, etc.

Reciprocal Platforms : r

... places where sooth and soothe meet
Muriel Rukeyser, *THE LIFE OF POETRY,* Current Books, NY; Paris Press edition, 1996.

The Stark Effect: Johannes Stark, 1919 Nobel Prize winner in physics for work with light spectral lines and related contributions to quantum physics.

During the post-war decade, when speaking of those killed by ww ɪɪ , *rest in pieces* was a phrase commonly used to replace *rest in peace.*

Noctivagate, vague nocturnal wanderings and digressions.

A "blind" renga, written with the poet George Kalamaras in 2005, appears on pages 38–46 of this poem.
On pages 38–41, Mr. Kalamaras provides the 7-7 syllable couplets; on pages 43–46, he provides the 5-7-5 syllable lines.

A River Vagus: Affecting heartbeat, breath, hearing, speech, digestion, perspiration, etc., the Vagus nerve begins in the brain and extends to the solar plexus.

Rendition: Word used by the Bush administration (11/05) for an "outsourcing" process to gather information from detainees during the "war on terror"; detainees were flown to other countries where information could be collected. Torture.

Parallel Umbrella

...on a tightrope of syllables.
Amy Uyematsu, "Red Rooster, Yellow Sky," ***30 Miles from J-Town***, Story Line Press, 1991.

"When we are, death is not; and when death is, we are not," Epicures (341-270 BC).

Pages 51–57 in Parallel Umbrella are a collaboration between Sheila E. Murphy and Mary Rising Higgins.

ShoreTrace

A breeze from the next poem
has slipped into this one. (p106)
Chase Twichell, "Work Libido," *DOG LANGUAGE*, Copper Canyon Press, 2005

      passion
also is just
a bridge
Marina Tsvetayeva, "The Poem of the End," *POEMS FOR THE MILLENNIUM, Vol. I*, University of CA Press, 1995.

Pages 65–72 are a collaboration among John Tritica, Mary Rising Higgins, and Gene Frumkin. The three poets contributed discrete sections in the order named. For each section, five to six lines of twelve or seven syllables were provided by the poets. Finally, linescape was arranged, in order upon the page, by Higgins.

[Here there is still a big gap in my thinking. And I doubt whether it will be filled now.]
Ludwig Wittgenstein, *ON CERTAINTY*, Edited by G. E. M. Anscombe and G. H. von Wright, © 1962 Basil Blackwell, Harper Torchbooks edition, 1972.

photograph page 5 : *digital big boil*

photograph page 13 : *cloud vortex fractal*

photograph page 81 : *nonlinear thermal instability*

Singing Horse Press Titles

Charles Alexander, *Near Or Random Acts*. 2004, $15.00

Rae Armantrout, *Collected Prose*. 2007, $17.00

David Antin, *John Cage Uncaged Is Still Cagey*. 2005, $15.00

Julia Blumenreich, *Meeting Tessie*. 1994, $6.00

Linh Dinh, *Drunkard Boxing*. 1998, $6.00

Norman Fischer, *Success*. 1999, $14.00

Norman Fischer, *I Was Blown Back*. 2005, $15.00

Phillip Foss, *The Ideation*. 2004, $15.00

Phillip Foss, *Imperfect Poverty*. 2006, $15.00

Eli Goldblatt, *Without a Trace*. 2001, $12.50

Mary Rising Higgins, *)cliff TIDES((*. 2005, $15.00

Mary Rising Higgins, *)joule TIDES((*. 2007, $15.00

Lindsay Hill, *Contango*. 2006, $14.00

Karen Kelley, *Her Angel*. 1992, $7.50

Karen Kelley, *Mysterious Peripheries*. 2006, $15.00

Kevin Killian & Leslie Scalapino, *Stone Marmalade*. 1996, $9.50

Hank Lazer, *The New Spirit*. 2005, $14.00

McCreary, Chris & Jenn, *The Effacements / a doctrine of signatures*. 2002, $12.50

David Miller, *The Waters of Marah*. 2002, $12.50

Andrew Mossin, *Epochal Body*. 2004, $15.00

Paul Naylor, *Playing Well With Others*. 2004, $15.00

Gil Ott, *Pact*. 2002, $14.00

Heather Thomas, *Practicing Amnesia*. 2000, $12.50

Rosmarie Waldrop, *Split Infinities*. 1998, $14.00

Lewis Warsh, *Touch of the Whip*. 2001, $14.00

These titles are available online at www.singinghorsepress.com,
or through Small Press Distribution, at (800) 869-7553, or online at www.spdbooks.org.